The Shepherd Spy

and other plays for Christmas

Angie McEvansoneya

Onwards and Upwards Publishers
3 Radfords Turf
Cranbrook
Exeter
EX5 7DX
United Kingdom
www.onwardsandupwards.org

Copyright © Angie McEvansoneya 2018

The right of Angie McEvansoneya to be identified as the author of this work has been asserted by the author in accordance with the Copyright, Designs and Patents Act 1988.

All rights reserved.

No part of this publication may be reproduced or transmitted in any form or by any means, electronic or mechanical, including photocopy, recording or any information storage and retrieval system, without permission in writing from the author or publisher.

This first edition published in the United Kingdom by Onwards and Upwards Publishers (2018).

ISBN: 978-1-78815-677-6
Cover design: LM Graphic Design

Printed in the United Kingdom.

Contents

Preface 5

The Shepherd Spy 7

A Star is Born 17

The Nativity – A Mouse-Eye View 27

What Can I Give Him? 35

The Dream – A Play for Christmas 45

The Time Travellers 51

Good News Broadcast – Israeli TV, December 25th, 0000 59

Welcome to My House 71

The Donkey and the King 79

Beyond the Star 89

Christmas – The Real Story 97

Good News – Great Joy 108

Preface

As a newly qualified teacher, many years ago, my enthusiasm knew no bounds. I ended up in one staff meeting, much to the relief of the other teachers, volunteering to produce the Christmas play. To say I was inexperienced was putting it mildly, but we got through.

I have no recollection now as to what the children did – I vaguely remember that many of them had costumes representing various parts of the world and I'm sure if it had been a complete disaster it would be firmly etched on my memory.

More recently, I have written and produced a play for our church children's group most Christmases, representing the story of Jesus' birth as it happened and sticking, as nearly as possible, to the original accounts that we find in the Gospels of Matthew and Luke.

Most children today have only a very limited knowledge of what Christmas is really about. By actually taking part in a nativity play, the story can become a central part of the children's memories of Christmas.

Every one of the plays in this book presents a different slant on the Christmas story, with the author's licence as to some of the surrounding details. So we look at the story through different eyes, whether those of mice, a young spy of Herod's, the national news channel, the stars and so on.

Each of these plays has been tried and tested, some more than once. Almost without exception they have been performed in a small church building with a small stage and no curtains or spotlights.

For most groups, putting on a nativity play is extra to everything else that is going on around Christmas and time is very limited. These plays are written with that in mind. Time needed for rehearsing the whole group is kept to a minimum, although several of the plays require extra rehearsals for a limited number of children who have spoken parts. Most of the action is done by miming with a narrator (or multiple readers) telling the story. This also means that a wide age range of children can be involved with the older ones doing the reading parts. In addition, the number taking part is flexible; animals can be added to the stable, pages/attendants can be added for the wise men and so on.

I trust you will find this book a useful resource for your group/class and enjoy producing the plays as much as I have.

The Shepherd Spy

The Shepherd Spy is huge fun to produce. King Herod is visited by the wise men; when they leave to go to Bethlehem, he calls a page boy to spy on the people in Bethlehem and the wise men, and find out what is going on.

There are several characters with quite a few lines to learn. Extra rehearsals are definitely needed for those with the main speaking parts. The cast list is long, but many of the parts have just one or two lines. The jester needs to be someone with some sort of gymnastic or circus skills. He/she adds a bit of humour to the first part of the play.

The play follows closely the Bible text from Matthew's Gospel, surmising that Jesus was probably nearly two years old before the wise men reached Bethlehem and that they found Mary and the child in a house.

Ideally, a good-size stage with lighting and curtains is needed, but it is not essential. The first time *The Shepherd Spy* was produced, it was on a very small stage with no special lighting effects. It can be done!

CAST

Narrator

Speaking Parts

Herod
Jester *(needs to be able to do cartwheels, juggle or similar)*
Messenger
Wise man 1
Wise man 2
Wise man 3
Priest
Benjamin
Seller 1
Seller 2
Seller 3
Shepherd (Matthew)
Bible reader
Innkeeper

Non-speaking Parts

Mary
Joseph
Herod's servants
Teacher of the Law
Extra market sellers and crowd (any number)
Other shepherds
Shepherd boy
Angels

SCENE ONE
Herod's Throne Room

(HEROD is sitting on his throne, his SERVANTS in attendance, JESTER doing some sort of acrobatics.)

HEROD   *(in foul mood)* Enough of this tomfoolery. Tell me some jokes to sooth my nerves.

JESTER	All right, all right, but don't go off the deep end this time – you might get wet! Deep end – see? Roman baths – wet? *(shrugs)* Oh, never mind. Listen to this. What's the difference between camels and boiled potatoes?
HEROD	I don't know. What *is* the difference between camels and boiled potatoes?
JESTER	You can't mash camels!

(ALL groan.)

Try this one. What's the difference…

HEROD	*(angrily)* Enough! Any more of this and you'll end up as a boiled potato. Now, out of my sight.

(Exit JESTER. HEROD puts his head in his hands.)

What's wrong with me today? I have that sinking feeling, as though something bad is about to happen.

(Enter MESSENGER.)

I must be…

MESSENGER	Sire, there are three men at the door who say they are astronomers from a distant country. They say they are looking for a king and were directed to your palace.
HEROD	*(angrily)* A king! What king? I am the only king round here.
MESSENGER	They said, "The King of the Jews…"
HEROD	*(even angrier)* What!
MESSENGER	They seem to be very rich and their camels are laden with gifts.
HEROD	*(rubs hand together)* Well, show them in.

(Exit MESSENGER, bowing.)

    Maybe *they* can tell me something to make me feel better.

(Enter WISE MEN and MESSENGER.)

MESSENGER   The astronomers from the East, sire. *(turning to WISE MEN)* Sirs, this is the great King Herod, king of all Judea.

(WISE MEN bow.)

HEROD   Welcome to my palace, friends. I hear you study the stars. Tell me, what's in my stars for me today?

WISE MAN 1   We do not have the power to tell the future. We study the stars as a science.

WISE MAN 2   Back in our own country we saw the biggest star that has ever appeared. It is bigger and brighter than any other.

WISE MAN 1   Our ancient manuscripts tell us that such a star will appear and herald the coming of a king who will be greater than your King David. He will be the King of the Jews, the Messiah.

HEROD   *(angry)* You lie! There is no such child born here. *(to MESSENGER)* Call the priests and teachers of the law at once.

(Exit MESSENGER.)

(Enter PRIEST and TEACHER OF THE LAW. They kneel down in front of HEROD.)

    (to PRIEST and TEACHER OF THE LAW) Well, you know the Scriptures. What do they say about a Messiah being born? Speak! Don't just kneel there grovelling.

PRIEST In Bethlehem in Judea, sire. That is where the prophet Isaiah tells us the Messiah will be born.

HEROD *(with emphasis)* So! One who will usurp my authority... *(pause)* But wait, what do astronomers want with a baby Messiah?

WISE MAN 3 We have come to worship him, your majesty. But we must hurry to Bethlehem if that is where the prophet said the Messiah was to be born. It is nearly two years now since the star first appeared. He may not still be in Bethlehem.

HEROD Very well, go to Bethlehem, find your Messiah, then come and tell me where he lives. I would like to worship him too.

(Exit WISE MEN, bowing as they go.)

(claps twice, speaks loudly) Boy! Where's that boy, Benjamin? Never around when I need him.

(Enter BENJAMIN.)

BENJAMIN *(bowing)* You called, sire?

HEROD Yes, a job for you of great importance. I need a spy in Bethlehem. No one will suspect a boy like you. Dress up as a shepherd or something and see what you can find out about a baby Messiah – probably nearly two years old. You will be well paid if you are successful.

BENJAMIN Yes, sire. Thank you, sire. What do you intend to do?

HEROD That's my business. Now get out... and don't fail me.

(Exit BENJAMIN.)

SCENE TWO
In Bethlehem

(MARKET SELLERS, SHEPHERDS and CROWD mingling around.)

SELLER 1　　Oranges, ripe oranges from Jaffa. Who'll buy my oranges?

(Enter BENJAMIN.)

SELLER 2　　Figs from the Mount of Olives. Who'll buy...

SELLER 3　　Fresh fish from Galilee.

(Someone goes up and smells the fish and makes a face. SELLER 3 pushes him away and sees Benjamin.)

　　　　　　Hello, young shepherd. You're new to Bethlehem, aren't you? We've not seen you here before.

BENJAMIN　　You're wrong. I live here, but I'm looking for a new job. Do you know of a shepherd needing a boy – handsome, strong and ready for anything?

SELLER 3　　Well, Matthew there *(points)* is short-handed. *(calls out)* Here, Matthew, could you do with another shepherd boy?

MATTHEW　　Maybe, if he's good at his trade. Come here, boy, let me look at you. *(looks Benjamin up and down)* Your skin is very white for someone who has spent his life on the hills looking after the sheep.

BENJAMIN　　I... er... I have poor skin. I don't tan easily.

MATTHEW　　Well, I do need more help, as it happens. Come with me.

(Exit BENJAMIN and MATTHEW.)

SCENE THREE
On the Hillside

(SHEPHERDS and BENJAMIN are sitting around a fire. The NARRATOR is standing to the side of the stage.)

MATTHEW   It's going to be a cold night tonight. Reminds me of the night we heard the angels.

BENJAMIN   Angels? You must have been dreaming. *(aside)* This is great. I could be on to something here. Wait until Herod hears this.

MATTHEW   No, honest as I sit here. It was angels, I tell you. Come here and I'll tell you the whole story. It began…

(Close curtains or dim the lights on stage, and light up BIBLE READER and BENJAMIN, who comes forward to listen to him. SHEPHERDS exit.)

B. READER   When Emperor Caesar Augustus ordered a census to be taken throughout the Roman Empire…
(continues reading from Luke 2:3-18)

(The play continues in mime as BIBLE READER reads the passage in Luke's Gospel, allowing time for action. BENJAMIN stands to one side, watching the action.)

The scenes are as follows:

1. JOSEPH and MARY'S journey to Bethlehem *(coming from back of hall to allow time for the stage to be set for the nativity scene)*.

2. Nativity scene with MARY, JOPSEPH and the baby in the manger.

(Clear nativity scene, set scene for shepherds.)

3. SHEPHERDS on the hillside and ANGELS *(SHEPHERDS need to exit ready to come on again)*.

(Re-set nativity scene.)

4. SHEPHERDS visit the manger.

(Curtain closed or lights off stage, and some lighting put on front of house.)

5. Shepherds telling the street sellers *(scene in front of a curtain or on floor level)*.

(Spotlight back on BIBLE READER and BENJAMIN.)

BENJAMIN   But who was the baby?

B. READER   He was the one spoken of by the prophets hundreds of years before all this happened.

BENJAMIN   You mean the baby was the Messiah?

B. READER   You need to see for yourself. The family is still in Bethlehem. Go to the Inn of the Nine Camels. Ask there if they know where Joseph the carpenter is now living.

BENJAMIN   Thank you, I will. *(goes to centre stage, rubs hand together)* Herod should pay me double for this.

(Exit BENJAMIN.)

SCENE FOUR
Outside the Inn

(The first part of this scene could be done in front of curtain or on floor level.)

(Enter BENJAMIN.)

BENJAMIN   *(looks up)* Inn of the Nine Camels – this is it! We'll see what the Innkeeper has to say.

(Knocks on door. If curtain, INNKEEPER could appear from behind, otherwise can come from back of stage.)

INNKEEPER   Hello, what can I do for you?

BENJAMIN   I'm looking for Joseph the carpenter. I believe he has a young son. I love children and I...

INNKEEPER   That's strange! You're the second to ask for that family today. Have you been watching the stars too?

BENJAMIN   Stars. So it's them, Herod's visitors...

INNKEEPER   Herod? You mean King Herod?

BENJAMIN   *(hurriedly)* No, at least... oh, forget it. Just tell me where I can find Joseph the carpenter.

INNKEEPER   Behind the carpenter's shop in Isaac Street. That way. *(points to back of hall)*

(Exit BENJAMIN, running to back of hall. Exit INNKEEPER.)

15

SCENE FIVE
Inside the House

(MARY and CHILD in position – ideally a 2-year-old to play part of Jesus.)

B. READER   And what of the Wise Men who visited Herod? *(reads Matthew 2:9-11)*

(Play continues again with mime: WISE MEN enter from back of hall while Scripture is being read.)

(Enter BENJAMIN, furtively, from back of hall.)

BENJAMIN   *(having nearly reached stage)* That's got to be the place. Those astronomers have gone into the house. They've bowed as they would to a king. Herod must have changed his mind and come already to see the child. *(creeps up closer)* No, there's no sign of Herod here. Who are they bowing to? They look more like they're worshipping. *(closer)* It's him! It's the Messiah! Now I see it. Herod didn't want to worship the child, he wanted to get rid of him and I would have been a part of it. I'm not going back to Herod. This is where I want to be. *(goes up to child and kneels down)*

A Star is Born

There is to be a contest of all the stars in the galaxy, as God (the Master) seeks a star that is bright enough to be the Nativity star. The story aims to show that helping others and putting them first is God's best way for us.

There is not a huge amount of movement and it is very possible to perform this play on a small stage.

It requires a small group of children who can spend time in rehearsals apart from the rest. The nativity scene is static, so children doing these parts just need to know their positions.

As long as there are enough children for the basic parts, any number can take part as extra stars and also as animals in the nativity scene.

The narrator's part could be shared amongst several children, done by one very good reader or by an adult. The narrator needs to be positioned away from the main action.

Some lighting is needed, particularly for the last scene. A spotlight is ideal, but it can be done with just house lights switched full-on at the appropriate time.

A curtain would be good, but again, is not essential.

CAST

Narrator

Speaking Parts

STARS
Twinkle
Glitter
Shooting Star
Falling Star
Shiner

Non-speaking Parts

STARS
Starlet
Other stars

Mary
Joseph
Shepherds
Wise men
Animals and angels,
according to number of
children in group

(NARRATOR standing to the side of the stage.)

NARRATOR   Many years ago, up in the galaxy, far away from anywhere, the stars gathered together for a meeting called by their Master – the creator of the universe. In the stars' changing room, Twinkle, Glitter and Shiner, along with many of the other stars, are busy shining themselves up, ready for the Master's meeting.

SCENE ONE
In the Stars' Changing Room

(The STARS are getting ready for the Master's meeting, doing hair, looking in mirrors, etc.)

TWINKLE	Hurry up, Glitter. We'll be late.
GLITTER	I can't think what all the fuss is about.
SHINER	You know what the Master's orders are – every star has to be at the meeting. He's got something special to say.
TWINKLE	And we're to look our best
GLITTER	What is this special meeting about?
SHINER	No one knows, but it must be very important for the Master to call every star in the galaxy.
TWINKLE	And when the Master calls a meeting, we must all obey.

(Enter SHOOTING STAR from back of hall, pretending to shoot as she goes.)

	Oh, goodness. What's this? Whoever are you?
SHOOTING	I'm a shooting star. *(bows)* At your service. Shoot around the galaxy, I do.
GLITTER	You'd better get ready quickly – the meeting is very soon.
SHOOTING	What meeting? I've only just shot in.
GLITTER	The meeting the Master has called for all the stars.
SHOOTING	Oh no! I forgot! I was busy…
SHINER	*(groaning)* We know! Shooting around the galaxy.
SHOOTING	How did you know? Here, give me that mirror, I must get ready.

(Enter FALLING STAR from the back of the hall, falling down a few times as she goes.)

TWINKLE	Now who is this coming?

(FALLING STAR reaches stage.)

GLITTER	And who might you be?
FALLING	Just a falling star. But am I too late for the meeting?
SHINER	No, don't worry. You just have time to get ready.
TWINKLE	No, she hasn't. We must go now or we'll be late.

(Exit all except FALLING STAR.)

FALLING	Wait for me.

(Exit FALLING STAR, falling a few times.)

NARRATOR And so the stars gathered together – big and small, shiny and dull, from every corner of the galaxy.

The Master, Creator God, was there in all his splendour, making even the brightest star look dim. He looked around lovingly at all the stars he had made.

He was searching for one star in particular, but, as yet, not one of them was ready for the work he had for it to do. "I need a special star," he said, "for a very special mission. It is to be the brightest star in the galaxy. But first she must find the secret of brightness. You all have three days and then we will meet here again."

The stars went away, wondering what this special mission might be. Each one began to think how she would find the secret of brightness.

SCENE TWO
A Quiet Spot Somewhere in the Galaxy

(Enter GLITTER, SHOOTING STAR, TWINKLE, FALLING STAR and SHINER.)

GLITTER   What did you think of that?

TWINKLE   We are all going to have to work really hard to find the secret of brightness.

SHOOTING   I will dash around the galaxy. I'm the fastest. It should be easy for me. See you soon!

(Exit SHOOTING STAR, shooting as she goes.)

FALLING   Who does she think she is? She'll be so busy dashing around that she won't stop long enough to find out any secret.

SHINER   That's true. What do you think the rest of us should do? We've only got three days.

GLITTER   We could all go in different directions to look and then come back in time to get ready for the Master's next meeting. The secret must be hidden somewhere in the galaxy.

TWINKLE   That's a great idea. Glitter, you go that way. Shiner, you go there. Falling Star, you go towards the north and I'll go south.

FALLING   But I can't go very fast. I keep falling over.

TWINKLE   Don't worry, you have three whole days.

SHINER   Come on, let's get going.

(ALL exit in different directions.)

NARRATOR	And so the stars all went off in different directions, trying to find the secret of brightness. For nearly three days they looked high and low – in corners, holes and even outside their own galaxy. The star movement was something to behold. Never had such activity been seen from the earth at one time.
	Every star was sure she would be the only one to find the secret, but it was nowhere to be found. So their imaginations began to work double time. Some thought a good polish would be the best thing to do, while others decided that jewels would help, or maybe glittery new clothes. Each one returned to the dressing room with their own ideas to get ready for the Master's meeting. They all arrived, except one – Glitter was missing.

SCENE THREE
In the Stars' Dressing Room

(Enter ALL STARS except GLITTER.)

TWINKLE	Are we all here? Let's get ready. We don't want to be late.
SHINER	I wonder what the special job is that the Master has for one of us.
SHOOTING	It's got to be something very important. Anyway, I think I'm in with a chance. All that energy I've used shooting around has charged up my batteries. Look at me now. *(twirls around)*

FALLING	I didn't get very far. I kept falling over. But I do have a plan. Look at this polish I found – the very best. I'm going to use that.
TWINKLE	I got a new dress. Look at this – shining or what? *(twirls around)*
SHINER	It's OK, but look at my new necklace... Wait a minute, where's Glitter?

(ALL look around.)

FALLING	Glitter, where are you?
TWINKLE	She's going to be late. What shall we do? We can't go and see the Master without Glitter.
SHINER	We will have to if she doesn't come soon. It would be very rude not to be there on time.
TWINKLE	I suppose it's her fault for being late.
SHOOTING	Maybe she's got lost, or she could be hurt. Shall I go and look for her?
SHINER	That will make you late too. Come on, we must go.

(ALL exit.)

(ALL STARS, except GLITTER and the STARLET, need to be positioned on stage, but in as much darkness as possible.)

NARRATOR	Every star was excited, each one thinking they had found the secret of brightness. There was a buzz of excited voices as the Master entered. But somehow, as he stood there in all his shining glory, all their thoughts of being the very best and shiniest seemed to fade.

The stars all bowed low before their Master – the creator of the universe. Twinkle and Shiner felt just a bit guilty that they had not waited for Glitter. Shooting Star felt bad because she had not gone out to look for her. They felt very small, insignificant stars in the presence of the Master.

He looked around him with great love and pleasure. Each one had a beauty of her own and each one was the work of his hands, created back at the beginning of time. But he had, too, a hint of sadness. There was not one star there that shone quite brightly enough for the job he had in mind.

It had to be a very special brightness – good enough to herald the birth of his one and only Son into the world. The Master's excitement knew no bounds. His Son, to be born into humanity – he wanted the world to know and this star was to be the first message he would send.

SCENE FOUR
At the Master's Meeting

(Lights on, to light up stage showing ALL STARS. Enter GLITTER from behind the other stars, wearing a shining costume.)

NARRATOR	Suddenly there was a noise from the back of the crowd of stars…
GLITTER	*(breathless)* Am I late? I'm sorry, Master, I was delayed.
TWINKLE	Glitter, where have you been? What's happened?
SHINER	You look different. You're shining more and more.

FALLING	Glitter, you look beautiful!
SHOOTING	Wow! What has happened?
GLITTER	I looked and looked for the secret of brightness, but I found nothing. I was in a far off, dark place when I heard a faint voice. It was a tiny starlet. She was in trouble – she had lost her way and was hurt. I knew I had to get back for the meeting, but I couldn't leave the starlet there. So I stopped and helped her, even though I knew I would be late. Here she is.

(STARLET comes forward from behind other stars.)

                    She wanted to come to the Master's meeting too.

NARRATOR   All the stars stared as the tiny starlet stepped forward, but the Master just smiled. In Glitter he had found a star who didn't even realise she had become brighter as she helped another star. Here was the secret – it was not what the stars did to themselves that was important, but what they did for others.

                    And so it was, that on a special night, and for many nights after that, a star shone in the sky so brightly that is was seen by wise men far away from Israel, a star that stayed above the sky in Bethlehem.

(Pause for nativity scene to be set.)

(Stars arrange in semi-circle at back of scene with GLITTER in centre.)

NARRATOR   What lay beneath the star? Not a palace or a stately home, but a noisy stable, animals sharing with a couple and their newborn baby who lay asleep in a manger, shepherds kneeling beside the manger and wise men, who had travelled across many countries to worship the child who was to be the Saviour of the world.

All Heaven rejoiced on that night and the Master, the creator of the universe, must have looked down with delight to see his plan of salvation beginning to unfold.

The Nativity – A Mouse-Eye View

Alongside the presentation of the Nativity in this play, there is a family of mice living in the stable. They are fascinated by all that is going on in Jerusalem and especially in the stable.

The better your facilities, the easier this is to produce, but the play was originally done with very basic small staging, no lights, curtains or special effects.

Some thought is needed as to the placing of the mouse hole. Ideally it needs to be below stage level. A large stage could take the Nativity scene on one side and the mouse hole on the other. Some of the action during the play takes place on floor level. The mouse hole needs to be separate from that.

Extra rehearsals are needed for those with speaking parts. Things can be simplified by leaving out the angel dance which will obviously also need choreographing.

Use of lights and curtains would help with the effects and enable simpler scene changing, but they are not essential. It depends what facilities are available.

CAST

Speaking Parts

Reader
Innkeeper's wife
Maid (or boy)

MOUSE FAMILY
Mother mouse
Father mouse
Child mouse 1
Child mouse 2

Miming Parts

Mary
Joseph
Shepherds
Wise men

Dancers

Several angels

SCENE ONE
Outside the Inn

(Enter CHILD MOUSE 1 and CHILD MOUSE 2 running from the back of the hall, pursued by the INNKEEPER'S WIFE waving a broom.)

INN. WIFE Get out of my inn. How do you think I can get my baking done for so many visitors with you chasing around my feet? I'll be getting complaints about vermin.

(MICE escape into hole, panting.)

(reaches stage) And if you come back, I'll have you for soup. *(exit down centre hall muttering)* All these visitors to Bethlehem and I'm left to get rid of mice as well. What is the world coming to?

SCENE TWO
In the Mouse Hole

MOTHER M.   Wherever have you two been?

CHILD M. 1   We went to see what all the noise and excitement was about.

CHILD M. 2   There are people everywhere. I've never seen such crowds. We had to be careful that no one trod on us.

FATHER M.   There's never been so many people in Bethlehem. I've heard all the inns are full and there are still people pouring in through the gates, humans everywhere.

MOTHER M.   They'll be putting people to sleep in the stable next.

FATHER M.   *(laughs)* I don't think humans would sleep in a stable.

CHILD M. 2   It's too smelly.

CHILD M. 1   It's too noisy.

CHILD M. 2   They wouldn't like us around, for a start.

FATHER M.   I'm going to see what's happening… Wait a minute, strangers are coming into the stable. Keep quiet and watch.

SCENE THREE
In the Stable

(Stable is empty at this point except for a stool. Enter from back of hall MAID with lantern, MARY, JOSEPH and INNKEEPER'S WIFE. Stop just short of the stable.)

INN. WIFE   Will this do? It's the only space I have left that I can think of.

(MARY and JOSEPH shown into stable, led by MAID guiding with lantern. JOSEPH guides MARY to stool and helps her sit down.)

    There, I'll leave you now. I'll keep the animals outside tonight. You'll be warm and quiet here.

(Exit INNKEEPER'S WIFE with MAID.)

SCENE FOUR
In the Mouse Hole

MOTHER M.   Well, what do you think of that?

CHILD M. 1   The lady looks very kind.

CHILD M. 2   I think she's pretty and the man is looking after her so nicely.

FATHER M.   These people don't seem to mind being put in the stable to sleep. I'm going out to the fields where it's quieter. Something feels strange about tonight.

MOTHER M.   We'll all come.

(ALL MICE come out of hole and notice the star positioned to appear behind stable. MICE position on floor level by stage.)

SCENE FIVE
In the Fields

(A reading from Luke's Gospel or from a children's Bible story book, while scene mimed with SHEPHERDS and ANGELS. SHEPHERDS then exit down the hall, while angels remain on stage for some sort of dance – this is optional. This is all watched by the MICE. ANGELS exit after dance.)

MOTHER M. I could have sworn those were angels.

FATHER M. Of course they were angels. The real question is – what were angels doing talking and singing to shepherds?

CHILD M. 1 Those shepherds were frightened, weren't they?

CHILD M. 2 They looked more scared than that lady who saw me when she was making bread the other day.

CHILD M. 1 *(laughs)* You made her run, didn't you?!

MOTHER M. Shall we follow the shepherds and see where they go?

FATHER M. Yes, come on or we'll lose them when they get into the crowd.

(Exit MICE.)

SCENE SIX
At the Stable

(In place are MARY sitting on stool, JOSEPH standing and the manger. Enter a SHEPHERD from back of hall. When near front, beckons to others. All climb on to stage and kneel at manger.)

(Enter MICE from back of hall.)

FATHER M.   *(from about halfway down hall)* It's our stable they've gone into. What do you think it all means?

CHILD M. 1   Can I go and see what's happening?

MOTHER M.   Yes, you go, then come back and tell us.

(CHILD MOUSE 1 creeps into stable, looks into manger, then runs back to other MICE.)

FATHER M.   What's the matter? You look like you've seen a ghost.

CHILD M. 1   *(panting)* It's a baby *(pause)* in our stable. Come and look.

(MICE go to their hole and look from there.)

CHILD M. 2   Those shepherds look like they're kneeling down to the baby.

FATHER M.   Maybe they just want to see it better.

MOTHER M.   No, they're bowing down like humans do when they are worshipping God.

(Enter WISE MEN from back of hall.)

CHILD M. 1   *(points towards WISE MEN)* Look, there are more humans coming towards the stable.

(WISE MEN reach front and go on to stage, present gifts and kneel down in front of manger.)

CHILD M. 2   They're posh. One's got a crown on.

MOTHER M.   They're giving presents to the baby. What funny things to give a baby. The first one looks like a lump of gold and that's incense in that jar. What do you think the other one is?

FATHER M.   If I didn't know better, I would say it was myrrh, but who would give myrrh to a baby?

(Enter the MAID, followed by the INNKEEPER'S WIFE from back of hall. When maid reaches the front, she leans on her broom.)

MOTHER M.   Hush now! Watch out! It's the innkeeper's wife coming.

―――――――――

SCENE SEVEN
Outside the Stable

(The previous scene remains where it is and this scene is acted on floor level in front of the stage.)

INN. WIFE   And what do you think you are doing, my girl?

MAID   I'm going to sweep the yard.

INN. WIFE   Sweep the yard, when there's so much to do in the inn? Besides, you were idling, not working.

MAID   *(looking up dreamily)* It's the stars. There's a great big one tonight.

INN. WIFE   Stop jabbering and come with me or the only stars you'll see are when I give you a box around the ears.

MAID   But look, there really is something strange in the sky tonight.

INN. WIFE	Haven't I told you, get on with your work. What do you think I pay you for? *(grabs MAID by the ear and drags her into the stable)*
MAID	*(as she's pulled)* Ow! I'm coming!

(When they have climbed on to stage, both say, 'Oh!' and kneel down.)

FATHER M.	Who is this baby? Shepherds and rich men all worship him.
MOTHER M.	I don't understand what's happening here tonight. Is it the baby that's making everything different?

What Can I Give Him?

The last verse of *In the Bleak Midwinter* reads, 'What can I give him, poor as I am?' These words are the sentiment of a Jewish slave boy who is owned by the wise men.

It can be done with a small group, if the animals in the stable and attendants for the wise men are omitted. Extra rehearsals are needed for the speaking parts.

It is possible to do this play on a small stage as there is not much movement involved. Curtains and lights are an added bonus, if they are available. Particularly effective would be for the curtains to be opened on to the stable scene (scene four), as the wise men enter from the back of the hall.

CAST

Speaking Parts

WISE MEN
Toman
Shinar
Barsan

Slave Boy
Herod

HEROD'S COURT
Attendant
Doorman
Advisor 1
Advisor 2

Miming Parts

Additional attendants
to wise men
Mary
Joseph
Animals

SCENE ONE
In the Astronomers' Work Room

(TOMAN sitting at table with book, SLAVE BOY in attendance.)

TOMAN   I can't understand it. There must be a record somewhere. Someone must have seen this huge star before. Here, boy, stop messing around and go and fetch Shinar and Barsan. They must have seen this huge star.

SLAVE BOY   *(bows)* Yes, sir. *(exit slowly)*

TOMAN   Get a move on. Hurry, it's important.

(Enter SLAVE BOY, BARSAN and SHINAR.)

SHINAR	What's all this rush and mystery? Can't I drink my cocoa in peace?
BARSAN	It had better be good. I was…
TOMAN	It's that huge star. You must have seen it. Come here.

(ALL go across to the window and look up.)

BARSAN	That can't be a star, it's too big.
SHINAR	What else can it be? Toman is right.
TOMAN	I know, but what can it mean?
SHINAR	Here, boy, bring the books here.

(SLAVE BOY picks up a book.)

No, not that one, that's last year's Beano Annual.

TOMAN	Try that one. It the book of wisdom from ancient Syria.

(ALL look at book.)

BARSAN	There's got to be something about it somewhere.
SLAVE BOY	Please sir, I know…
TOMAN	Be quiet, boy. Let's try the Egyptian writings.
SLAVE BOY	But sir, I really…
TOMAN	I told you to be quiet. *(raises his hand to hit him but is stopped by SHINAR)*
SHINAR	Wait a minute, you come from Israel, boy. What do you know?

SLAVE BOY	Please, sir, our ancient writings speak of a star and a king who is to be born for our people. Our prophets long ago promised that the Messiah would be the one to save us from our enemies. They said he would be greater than King David, our greatest king. The Messiah would be a sort of priest as well. But there will be sadness and sorrow coming to him.
BARSAN	A king, you say, to be born in Israel? This star must be the sign of his coming. *(slowly and thoughtfully)* Maybe we should go and see this great king.
TOMAN	Where should we go? To Jerusalem? That's where the Jews have their royal palace. I believe the present king is called Herod.
SHINAR	We'll need to take gifts with us, fit for a king. I have gold I could take. You can't give a king anything more valuable than that.
TOMAN	What else did you say about him, boy?
SLAVE BOY	That he would be a sort of priest as well as a king. Is that the bit you meant?
TOMAN	*(thoughtfully)* Yes. I think I'll take incense. That's what priests use for worship and prayer, isn't it?
SHINAR	What does that leave for me to take? I'm sure they'll have lots of fine clothes and Herod will have thought of everything else that he needs.
SLAVE BOY	Please, sir, maybe he needs something for his time of sadness and sorrow.
SHINAR	You mean he is going to die? I could take myrrh for his body in death. There is no finer myrrh than that produced in our country.

TOMAN	Well, boy, you have been very helpful. I will reward you by taking you with us. You will be the chief slave for the journey and be the guardian of the gifts.

SLAVE BOY	Thank you, sir.

(Exit WISE MEN.)

But what can I give him? I'm only a slave. I own nothing. I have nothing to take. I guess no one will notice me anyway, so it won't matter.

(Exit SLAVE BOY with head held down.)

SCENE TWO
In Herod's Palace

(HEROD on throne, ATTENDANT playing instrument. HEROD in foul mood.)

HEROD	Enough of this. You play all the wrong notes. I need a drink. Fetch one at once.

ATTENDANT	Yes, sire. At once, sire.

(Exit ATTENDANT, then re-enter carrying cup which he hands to HEROD.)

HEROD	*(drinks from cup)* That's better. I might almost manage to be in a good mood now, as long as you don't start making that terrible noise again. Where are my advisors? I'd like... *(loud knocking from offstage)* Now what? Am I to get no peace today?

(Enter DOORMAN.)

DOORMAN	I am here, sire, to announce the arrival of three men who look both rich and wise. Shall I let them approach, sire?
HEROD	By all means. Let them come in as long as they really are rich and have gifts for me.
DOORMAN	*(loudly)* Three men from a distant land to visit the great King Herod in his royal palace in Jerusalem.

(Enter WISE MEN.)

	(to WISE MEN) Please enter the royal presence.
SHINAR	*(bows to HEROD)* We are three men who study the stars and have travelled a long way to be here. My name is Shinar.
BARSAN	*(also bowing)* Barsan at your service, your majesty. We have seen a huge star in the sky and learned from your scriptures that it is a sign that a new king has been born.
TOMAN	*(steps forward and bows)* My name is Toman. We would like to congratulate you on the birth of a very special prince in your royal palace. We have come to worship him. We have brought…
HEROD	*(getting angry)* Prince! In my palace! What is this nonsense you are talking? There is no king here except me and no prince either. You are spies. You will be locked up until you talk some sense.
ATTENDANT	Please, sire, maybe you are being a bit hasty. Perhaps your advisors could help.
HEROD	Maybe you're right. Fetch them here at once.

(Exit ATTENDANT, return with ADVISORS.)

(to WISE MEN) Tell your story to these men. They are experts in our scriptures.

BARSAN	We noticed one night a star that had appeared that was much bigger than all the others. Our slave is one of your people. He told us what was spoken by your prophets many hundreds of years ago, that a great king will be born who will rescue his people, the Jews.
ADVISOR 1	This is true, but I'm sure it was not Jerusalem where he is to be born.
ADVISOR 2	That is right. Bethlehem is the place. *(turns to Herod)*

(WISE MEN talk among themselves.)

	Your majesty, this king is to be a descendant of our great King David. If he is such a king…
ADVISOR 1	You will have to guard your position, your majesty. One day he may take over the kingdom and you will end your days eating pig food.
HEROD	*(angrily)* That will never be. Here is my faithful attendant. Do you have any advice for me?
ATTENDANT	You could abdicate the throne now, sire. That would save a battle later on.
HEROD	*(angrily)* You fool! Get out of my sight! *(sweetly)* You men from afar, when did you first see the star?
SHINAR	It was many months ago. It has taken us all this time to travel here.
HEROD	Well, my advisors have convinced me about the truth of your story. I too would like to worship this new king. When you have found him, come back here and tell me where he is so I can go and worship him too.

TOMAN Of course, your majesty. Now please let us hurry to Bethlehem.

(Exit WISE MEN through hall, everyone else off stage right or left.)

SCENE THREE
At the Stable in Bethlehem

(Traditional stable scene with JOSEPH, MARY and BABY in manger, animals. Enter WISE MEN from back of hall in procession led by slave boy.)

SHINAR *(as nears the front of hall)* Look, the star is right here above us now. This must be the place.

TOMAN It doesn't look like the sort of place for a king.

BARSAN Never mind, we must follow the leading of the star. Here, slave boy, now is the time to give us our gifts for the king.

(ALL enter and present gifts and kneel at the manger, except the SLAVE BOY.)

TOMAN *(turns back to fetch SLAVE BOY)* Why have you stayed out here? You can come and see the baby too.

SLAVE BOY But I have nothing to give him. I have nothing of my own, not even a penny to lay on his crib.

TOMAN Come on inside. When you see the baby king, you'll know it's not the gifts we give him that count. He just wants to know that we will be his friend and loyal subjects in his kingdom.

SLAVE BOY You mean that I'm the gift? That's what I can give him – myself.

Hold scene for a group or whole congregation to sing 'In the Bleak Midwinter'.

The Dream – A Play for Christmas

Are we leaving Jesus out of Christmas? is the challenge of this play.

It is really a story read by the storyteller, with an angel's one-liner which must be loud and clear enough for the audience to hear. The storyteller needs to be an adult or maybe a much older child. Apart from him/her, this is a play that can be done with quite small children. The number in the cast can vary from as few as ten to twice that. It is adaptable according to the group/class size and number of figures in your Christmas crib scene.

The Dream is designed for minimal rehearsing and can be performed easily on a small stage. A spotlight on the crib scene would be ideal, but not essential. What is needed is a good-sized crib scene with a good number of different pieces.

One of its features is the costumes, representing as many countries as possible; amongst them could be – a cowboy, a red Indian, Indian (with sari), mid European (skirt, apron, sleeveless jacket), Welsh girl (the hat would be the giveaway!), Chinese in silk trousers and top, Japanese in kimono, London business man (suit and tie), Eskimo, etc. Some of the children may already have such costumes, others can be put together from a dressing-up box.

The aim is to bring the children on from different directions to show them coming from different corners of the world.

CAST

Children in costumes from all over the world
Angels (one speaking part)
Kevin
Storyteller

ALSO: a large crib scene with figures for the children to place in the stable as the play proceeds

---

SCENE ONE
In Kevin's Bedroom

(A bed in the corner, empty stable for crib scene on table in middle.)

(STORYTELLER in position at the side of the stage, KEVIN in bed.)

STORYTELL. It was Christmas Eve. Kevin lay in bed, staring up at the stars which he could see through the hole in his bedroom ceiling. There was the Great Bear – he knew that one. He wondered what Jesus' special star had looked like, the one that appeared over two thousand years ago, a star bigger and brighter than all the rest.

He pulled his thin blanket more tightly around him as a cold blast of wind came in through the hole. It seemed to be getting bigger, but there was no way that his parents could afford to mend it. He was used to being cold anyway. This night was no different.

Kevin thought of his friends, of their excitement hanging up their stockings, the expectation that they would be overflowing on Christmas morning with all sorts of good things. There was no point in Kevin hanging up a stocking, even if he had had one. His mum and dad did not have enough to feed the three of them, let alone be able to buy extras just because it was Christmas.

Kevin longed more than anything else for an orange. He had had one once when a boy at school did not want his. For a few moments Kevin thought he was in Heaven. He sucked every last drop of the juice that stuck to his fingers. He thought of the wonderful taste as he imagined his friends having oranges, and so much more, in their stockings and… But Kevin was asleep.

He woke with a start some time later. Was it a noise that had woken him or was it the lights he could see moving around in the darkness?

(KEVIN gets up and moves nearer to the stable.)

As he accustomed his eyes to the dark, he realised that there were children coming towards a point quite near to where he was now standing.

(Enter CHILDREN – one or two at a time.)

They came from every part of the world – from north, south, east and west. Many of them carried something in their hands. Kevin could not see what these were. In front of him was something that looked like a wooden box.

He looked again. It wasn't a box, it was a model of a stable, something like the one his teacher had told him about – the stable where Jesus was born.

(STORYTELLER reads slowly, and CHILDREN put each piece into place in the stable as their character is read out by the STORYTELLER. CHILDREN gradually form an arc behind the stable.)

>Yes, there was Mary...
>
>And Joseph...
>
>An angel...
>
>Three animals:
>
>>an ox...
>>
>>a donkey...
>>
>>a sheep...
>
>An angel...
>
>The shepherds...
>
>And the wise men with their gifts of gold, frankincense and myrrh...
>
>What did this all mean, Kevin wondered as he watched the children, all dressed in bright colours, from every continent – Africa, Europe, Asia, America, Australia. Was it to show that Jesus came for the whole world?
>
>Barely was the stable scene complete than angels began to appear, as if out of nowhere.

(Enter ANGELS.)

>Each one looked into the stable. Kevin wondered if any of these were among the angels who had sung to the shepherds on the night that Jesus was born.

(Enter final ANGEL.)

At last came one angel later than the rest. In the quiet of the night, her voice rang out loud and clear.

ANGEL Where is Jesus? They've left Jesus out of Christmas!

STORYTELL. There was a stunned silence, then chaos broke out – angels and children running all over the place looking for the missing and most important piece of the crib scene.

One angel came up to Kevin and took him back to his bed. Was this it? Was everything to be left in chaos?

The angel carefully lifted the corner of his thin pillow. There, under its folds, was the missing piece – Jesus in the manger. Kevin couldn't believe his eyes. He had never seen it before in his life. How did it get there?

(KEVIN puts figure into stable.)

At once the chaos stopped.

(ANGELS and CHILDREN kneel down around the crib – hold this position until end.)

Angels and children knelt down beside the stable and worshipped – not the tiny statue, but the eternal Lord Jesus who came as a baby on the first Christmas.

And that is when Kevin left them.

(KEVIN returns to bed.)

He crept back to his bed and the thin blanket, the hole in the ceiling... and sleep. *(pause)*

He woke early the next morning, feeling excited, although he knew that this day would be like any other in his house. He would still feel hungry and cold. But this morning something was different. He could feel it. Was it because he had learnt that stockings and all the rest weren't the important part of Christmas? The angel's words rang in his ears: 'They've left Jesus out of Christmas.' But why should he feel any different? It had all been a dream anyway.

(KEVIN gets up and begins to tidy bed.)

Kevin leant down to tidy his bed – well, just a bit of a tidy! There under his pillow, where the angel had shown him the figure of Jesus in the manger, was a one-pound coin. Kevin couldn't believe his eyes. This was enough for three big oranges – one each for his mum and dad and one for him. Was it all *really* a dream?

The Time Travellers

Two children are returning from a Christmas party. It is late and they fall asleep and begin to dream...

It would be effective to use floodlighting (not essential) and curtains, if they are available, so that the actual time-travelling could take place in front of the curtains while props, etc. are being put in place behind.

Just a small group, those with the speaking parts, are required to have extra rehearsals. The nativity parts are all mimed.

CAST

Girl

Boy

Alltime

Isaiah

Readers (can use just one or two readers or different readers for each reading)

Mary

Gabriel

Joseph

Shepherds

Angels

Wise Men

SCENE ONE
In the Sitting Room

(One side of the stage is set with a settee or two chairs. This stays in position throughout play.)

(CHILDREN enter excitedly from the back of the hall waving balloons.)

GIRL   That party was great. Christmas parties are always special. I'm glad we all had a balloon at the end.

BOY   I liked the food, especially the cake.

GIRL   Did you see Paul spill his Coke? It went everywhere. It was a right mess!

BOY   Waste of Coke too.

(Clock chimes 11.00.)

	Wow, is it that late?
GIRL	I don't feel like going to bed yet. Let's sit here for a bit.

(BOTH sit down on chairs/settee.)

BOY	Isn't it quiet?
GIRL	Do you think it was as quiet as this on the night Jesus was born – all peaceful, with the baby lying in the manger?
BOY	I don't think so with all those animals around.
GIRL	*(sleepily)* Wish we could have been there and seen the baby, like the shepherds did.
BOY	*(dreamily)* Yeah, would have been amazing…

(BOTH fall asleep – lights out.)

(Enter ALLTIME carrying a Bible, clock strikes 12.00, CHILDREN wake up.)

BOY	*(sees ALLTIME)* Who on earth are you?
ALLTIME	My name is Alltime and I've come to take you on a journey back in time.
BOY	Wow, where are we going?
ALLTIME	You both wanted to see the new-born baby Jesus, didn't you?
GIRL	Ooh, yes, and Mary and Joseph and the shepherds and the wise…
ALLTIME	Steady on. The story began long before that. It all started in a garden.
BOY	Was that the Garden of Eden?

ALLTIME	Yes, it's all here in the Bible. *(Open Bible and read the script here.)* Just after God made everything and saw how good it was, Adam and Eve disobeyed God, and the perfect world he had been so pleased with was spoilt. That was the beginning of sin.
GIRL	But didn't God know what was going to happen? Couldn't he have stopped it?
ALLTIME	He could, but he had chosen to give man a free will to choose what is right and what is wrong. He also had a plan, because he loves us. He sent his son, Jesus, to the earth to deal with the sin problem. Look, it's here in the book of Isaiah. *(shows CHILDREN Bible)* Better still, let's begin our journey back in time that I told you about. I'll take you back about two thousand seven hundred years to the time of Isaiah the prophet. Come and hold my hand, one on either side. Now close your eyes and…

(Lights out and sound effects for time travel.)

(Lights on and sound off. Enter ISAIAH and stand on opposite side of stage, holding scroll.)

	There. Are you both OK?
BOY	That was amazing. I don't feel as though I've travelled two thousand seven hundred years. But who is that? *(points at ISAIAH)*
ALLTIME	That is Isaiah the prophet. Listen to the message he has heard from God.
ISAIAH	*(Reads from scroll – Isaiah 40:1-5.)*

(Exit ISAIAH.)

ALLTIME   That was what God promised seven hundred years before Jesus was born. But we must hurry on if you are to see Jesus in the manger. Hold my hands again and we'll move on in time to about nine months before Jesus was born.

(CHILDREN hold ALLTIME'S hand. Lights out and time-travel sound effects.)

(Lights on and sound off. ALLTIME and CHILDREN stand at the side of the stage. Enter READER and stand on opposite side of the stage.)

(Enter MARY and sit centre stage.)

(Enter GABRIEL. MARY and GABRIEL mime while story is being read.)

READER   *(Read Luke 1:26-35,38.)*

(Exit MARY, GABRIEL.)

BOY   If Mary lived at Nazareth, how come Jesus was born in Bethlehem?

ALLTIME   You need to hear the next bit of the story to know the answer to that. We are going to travel on just a few months.

(CHILDREN hold ALLTIME'S hands, lights out and time-travel sound effects.)

(Lights on, manger and stool in place. ALLTIME and CHILDREN hold position.)

(Enter MARY and JOSEPH. MARY sits by manger with JOSEPH behind. Hold this position during reading.)

READER   *(Reads Luke 2:1-7.)*

(Close scene using curtains and/or lights.)

SCENE TWO
In the Shepherds' Field

(ALLTIME and CHILDREN in same position.)

(Enter SHEPHERDS and sit around fire.)

(While reading going on: SHEPHERDS mime scene, with ANGELS entering at appropriate time.)

READER   (Reads Luke 2:8-15.)

(Curtain and/or blackout.)

SCENE THREE
In the Stable

(Re-set stable scene with MARY and JOSEPH in position, also ALLTIME and CHILDREN.)

(Enter SHEPHERDS and kneel around manger during reading.)

READER   (Read Luke 2:16-20.)

(ALL hold positions.)

GIRL   I thought someone else came to visit baby Jesus.

ALLTIME   Yes, there were three wise men who saw a special star that appeared when Jesus was born. They were expecting to see a prince so they went to the palace in Jerusalem.

BOY   But Jesus was born here in Bethlehem.

ALLTIME   That's what King Herod's advisors told them. So they went to Bethlehem.

(Enter WISE MEN from back of hall, move slowly to front. While reading takes place, present gifts at manger, kneel or stand with SHEPHERDS to make a tableau.)

READER   *(Read Matthew 2:9-11.)*

(Lights out on manger scene. Boy and girl return to sleep on the settee.)

BOY   *(wakes up)* Oh, I'm stiff. I've got pins and needles in my legs.

GIRL   We must have fallen asleep. I've been dreaming and it was so real.

BOY   I dreamt we saw the new-born baby Jesus, just like you said you wanted to do.

GIRL   But, so did I. *(lights on manger scene)* Look!

Good News Broadcast – Israeli TV, December 25th, 0000

We are in the news studio of Israeli television in the year 0000, as well as out on location with local reporters. Much of the script (the studio and reporters' parts) can be read, although the more familiar they are with the script, the better. Other speaking parts need to be learnt. The play is suitable for a mixed age group, including teens, who could take the speaking parts.

There are a lot of scenes. A big stage could have the TV studio set up on one side. Scene changes would be easier if a curtain can be used, but it is possible to do the whole thing on a small stage with no curtain (it has been done!)

Also, lights could be used very effectively, but are not essential.

CAST

Speaking Parts	**Non-speaking Parts**
Announcer	Crowd in Bethlehem
NEWSCASTER	Shepherds
Benjamin	Gabriel
	Angels
REPORTERS	Mary
Reuben	Joseph
Simeon	Animals (optional)
Judah	
INNKEEPER	
Jacob	
Wise man 1	
Wise man 2	
Wise man 3	
Shepherd 1	
Shepherd 2	

SCENE ONE
In the News Studio

(Sound effect: intro for the BBC or ITV 10 o'clock news. ANNOUNCER and BENJAMIN are sitting at a desk.)

ANNOUNC. *(reads)* This is Israeli television bringing you the latest news from at home and around the Roman Empire. Here are the headlines:

- Inns full as crowds pour into the towns and cities to be counted.

- Astronomers from the east report sighting of a unique star.

- Shepherds on the hillside near Bethlehem report seeing a host of angels.

- Woman gives birth in a stable.

And here to bring you all the details of today's news is Benjamin of Emmaus.

BENJAMIN	*(reads)* Good evening. This is Benjamin of Emmaus bringing you today's news.

                The response to the Emperor's decree that everyone should return to his home town for the census of the people has brought an overwhelming people-movement, not seen since the days of Moses and the Exodus from Egypt. The town worst hit is Bethlehem in the territory of Judah. The innkeepers have run out of places for people to stay and the Governor has requested that all who have brought tents and bed-rolls with them should stay outside the town to relieve the overcrowding.

                We go over to Reuben, our reporter in Bethlehem, for the latest situation.

SCENE TWO
In the Centre of Bethlehem

(Enter CROWD milling about, REUBEN and INNKEEPER JACOB. REUBEN and JACOB move to front of stage.)

REUBEN   *(to audience)* Hello and welcome to the centre of Bethlehem where you can see behind me that the crowds are still jostling for somewhere to sleep.

(turn to INNKEEPER) With me I have Jacob, innkeeper of the Nine Camels Inn, right here near the Central Square. His inn has been full since early this afternoon.

Jacob, have you ever seen anything like this?

JACOB   It's just amazing! *(pause to rub hands together)* But very good for business.

REUBEN   Have you had to turn anyone away yet?

JACOB   Oh yes, lots of people. But there was one couple I hadn't the heart to turn away even though we were bursting at the seams. They had travelled all the way from Nazareth and she very near to giving birth. Due any time, I would say. She looked so tired; how could I, a good Jew, turn her away?

REUBEN   What did you do? Surely you didn't turn someone else out?

JACOB   I have this cave round the back of my inn. I put the animals in it when the inn is full. It was the only place I could think of. The couple were very happy to rest on the straw amongst the animals *(pause)* and I said I would only charge them half price.

REUBEN   Thank you, Jacob. I think we may have more on this story later.

This is Reuben handing you back to the studio.

SCENE THREE
Back in the Studio

(Studio set as before with ANNOUNCER and BENJAMIN at desk.)

BENJAMIN   *(reads)* It was announced today by three leading astronomers from the east that a new star has been sighted somewhere in the region of Jerusalem. It is said to be bigger than any star yet seen in the night sky and is clearly visible to the naked eye.

Simeon, our reporter in the east, is with the astronomers now.

SCENE FOUR
In the Astronomers' Sky-watching Lab

(Enter WISE MEN with SIMEON.)

SIMEON   *(comes to front of stage and speaks to audience)* I am in the sky-watching lab of these very eminent astronomers. We can see from here the star they have detected, clearly visible in the distance, possibly over the Jerusalem area. *(turns to WISE MAN 1)* Can I ask – when did you first see this extraordinary star?

WISE MAN 1   Just tonight. We still can't believe its size and capacity for light.

SIMEON   Might you have missed seeing it before?

WISE MAN 2   Impossible. We study the stars carefully every night. You don't even need an instrument to see this star. We can't possibly have missed seeing it before.

WISE MAN 3	It's a sign, don't you see? Your Israeli prophets spoke of a coming king who would be greater than your King David. Your Messiah must have come. That's the only explanation of this star that makes sense.
WISE MAN 2	This is no natural star. It's too big. It's got to be a sign from God.
SIMEON	What do you intend to do about it?
WISE MAN 1	We will travel to the palace of King Herod in Jerusalem. It's the obvious place to find a future king.
SIMEON	But Jerusalem is hundreds of miles away. You can't just drop everything and go, just like that.
WISE MAN 2	We've got to find this king, this Messiah. We feel it is more important than all the work we are doing here. We will be leaving as soon as we've found suitable gifts to take with us.
SIMEON	What gifts do you have in mind?
WISE MAN 3	They would have to be very special gifts if this really is the Messiah king spoken of by your prophets. I will take gold, that's a gift fit for any king.
SIMEON	You others, you could take jewels, crowns, anything like that.
WISE MAN 2	No. Looking at the writings of the prophets, this king is also some sort of a priest. I will take incense for him to offer in prayer.
WISE MAN 1	I feel something showing sorrow should be my gift. The prophet Isaiah spoke of the Messiah as one who would suffer. My gift will be myrrh in preparation for sadness to come.

SIMEON   Well, I would like to wish you every success for your journey from all of us at Israeli Television.

And now I will hand you back to the studio.

(Exit WISE MEN and SIMEON.)

SCENE FIVE
In the Television Studio

(Studio set as before with ANNOUNCER and BENJAMIN at the desk.)

BENJAMIN   Shepherds minding their own business, looking after their sheep on the hills outside Bethlehem, report the sighting of a talking angel, dazzling lights and a choir of singing angels.

These reports have yet to be verified, as no one else around saw or heard anything. However, experts have ruled out hallucination, as the sightings were by a group, not by an individual.

UFO experts have been to the alleged scene, but say that the shepherds' report bears no similarity with the normal characteristics of an unidentified flying object.

However, we will let the shepherds speak for themselves. We go now to Judah, our reporter on the hills outside Bethlehem.

SCENE SIX
On the Hillside Outside Bethlehem

(Shepherds' fire in centre of stage. Enter JUDAH with SHEPHERDS 1 and 2.)

JUDAH *(to the audience)* All is now quiet in the hills above Bethlehem. But earlier this evening, according to the shepherds, events led them to be scared out of their wits. I have here two of the shepherds concerned. *(to the SHEPHERDS)* Tell me, what did you see?

SHPEHERD 1 The first thing we saw was an angel and bright lights. Them lights were dazzling. It must have been something a bit like Moses saw when he met with God on Mount Sinai. Young Ishmael got out his phone and managed to get a video of the whole thing.

JUDAH Viewers, this is amazing! The following exclusive video footage shows these incredible events. The shepherds themselves will tell us what is happening.

(Enter other SHEPHERDS and sit around fire.)

SHEPHERD 1 We were sitting around as usual, trying to get warm, keeping watch over the flocks.

(Enter GABRIEL.)

Suddenly an angel appeared and spoke to us. He told us not to be afraid – he could see we were dead scared. Micah here went deathly white and fainted.

SHEPHERD 2 You didn't have to say that. I couldn't help it.

JUDAH What did the angel say next?

SHEPHERD 1	That he had good news for us which was going to bring joy to people everywhere. Now, here's the strange bit – he said that the Messiah had been born in Bethlehem this very day and, as proof that what he'd said was true, we'd find the baby lying in a manger. I ask you, who'd put a new-born baby in a manger?

(Enter ANGELS, stand behind SHEPHERDS.)

JUDAH	What's happening now?
SHEPHERD 2	It's all the other angels. I was just coming round, like, from fainting, when I heard this choir of angels. I thought my time had come and I'd gone into another world. So I pinched me-self and it hurt – so I knew it was real, like. The angels were singing praises to God – look, you can see them. I realised I wasn't scared anymore. I felt warm inside and excited, like.

(Exit GABRIEL and ANGELS.)

JUDAH	What happened next?
SHEPHERD 1	The angels went away and Ishmael switched off his phone. Suddenly it was very quiet. Even the sheep had stopped bleating. The boss said, "Let's go into the city and see if we can find the baby lying in the manger." Seemed like the right thing to do.
JUDAH	Is that where you are going now? What about your sheep?
SHEPHERD 2	We can't take them with us. Cause a right stir, like – a flock of sheep in Bethlehem in the middle of the night.
SHEPHERD 1	We figure, if the angel's message was from God, then God will take care of the sheep for a while.

(Exit SHEPHERDS.)

JUDAH   So, viewers, as the shepherds leave the hillside, I am returning you to the studio.

(Exit JUDAH.)

SCENE SEVEN
In the Studio

(Scene set as before with ANNOUNCER and BENJAMIN sitting at the desk.)

BENJAMIN   Reports that a woman has given birth to a baby amongst sheep and cattle in a stable and has laid him to sleep in a manger have yet to be confirmed. If true, this is highly irregular and will need to be investigated by Social Services, the NSPCC and other children's organisations.

I am told by my producers that we can go live again to the centre of Bethlehem. So it's over to Reuben, our reporter on the spot. *(speaks into another mic)* Reuben, what's happening now?

SCENE EIGHT
In the Stable

(On stage: MARY and JOSEPH with manger.)

(REUBEN is standing away from stable, possibly on floor level. SHEPHERDS enter from back of hall.)

REUBEN   It's now the middle of the night and most people have at least found somewhere to sleep, but there is still movement on the streets. It's a group of shepherds going towards the place where that innkeeper put the young couple who were about to have a baby.

(SHEPHERDS go into stable and kneel down.)

They're going inside the stable. Now I can't see any more. Just wait a minute and I'll catch them as soon as they come back out.

(SHEPHERDS exit stable.)

Here they are. *(goes up to SHEPHERDS)* Excuse me, can I ask what is going on here? What were you doing in the stable?

SHEPHERD 1   We've just seen it – I mean, him – the Messiah, just as the angel told us. He was lying in the manger all wrapped in cloth. There he was, all tiny and newborn.

SHEPHERD 2   Perfect he was, and his mum and dad looking so proud, like. Makes you want to sing out loud and jump for joy. I shall never forget this night for as long as I live.

REUBEN   Thank you, shepherds. Now I am handing you back to the studio.

(Exit ALL.)

―――――――――

SCENE NINE
In the Studio

(Scene as before with ANNOUNCER and BENJAMIN at desk.)

ANNOUNC.   We will leave you, the viewers, to decide. Is this the Messiah the world has been promised? Is this baby the Saviour of the world?

This is the end of the news on this extraordinary night – or is it just the beginning?

Welcome to My House

Suppose Jesus had been born in Lapland, or Uganda, or in Wales? The aim of this play is to show how Jesus was born in poverty, not in a palace surrounded by wealth and privilege. He did not even come to an area or age of comfortable surroundings.

There is not a lot of movement or acting in this play, but there are a few lines for most to learn. The narrator has a lot of lines and he/she could use a script, but should be very familiar with it, so as not to have to read it word for word.

The countries used in the script could be changed a bit according to the availability of costumes, which need imagination on the part of the costume department.

The most effective way to present this would be to have the action taking place in a space in front of the curtains and the nativity scene behind the curtains with Mary and Joseph. Animals could also be in the scene if enough children are available.

Note: If possible, the children from around the world come in from different directions to give the impression that they are coming from different parts of the world.

CAST

Speaking Parts

Reader
Narrator

CHILDREN FROM AROUND
THE WORLD

Eskimo
Chinese
Nomad
Russian
Austrian
Footballer
Welsh
Hawaiian
Ugandan
Arab
Turk
French

Non-speaking Parts

Mary
Joseph

SCENE ONE
Somewhere in the World!

Enter READER and NARRATOR.)

READER   (Read Matthew 2:1-2.)

NARRATOR   When the wise men went to visit Jesus, they were looking for a king, expecting to find him in a palace. They headed for Jerusalem and met Herod – not a good move!

We now enter the world of imagination. What if God had chosen his Son to be born somewhere else – in another country, in richer circumstances, at another time in history?

(Enter ESKIMO.)

Where would Jesus have lived? Would he have been welcomed there? What would it have been... Oh, hello, where have you come from?

ESKIMO   I come from Greenland.

NARRATOR   That's a long way away. What are you doing here?

ESKIMO   I have heard that a new king has been born. I would like to give him a welcome in my igloo. It's very warm inside and we have beautiful furs we could wrap him in.

NARRATOR   That's a very nice thought...

(Enter CHINESE.)

...but Jesus, the new king, was born a long way from Greenland. Hello, who are you?

(ESKIMO stands to one side.)

CHINESE   I am Lin Lang. I have come all the way from China. I heard that a new king has been born. I would like to give him a welcome in my home. If he is a king, he will need our very best silks to wrap him in and a nanny to care for him.

NARRATOR   But Jesus never had silks to wrap him in or a nanny to care for him.

(Enter NOMAD.)

Oh, here's someone very different. Where have you come from?

(CHINESE stands to one side.)

NOMAD I live in the Sahara Desert. I wonder if you can help me. I have come looking for the king who has been born. I would like to welcome him to my family's tent. My father is the chief of our tribe and we have the very best tent there is. We travel all over the place and he could visit his subjects with us. He needn't walk. We would give him our very best camel.

NARRATOR That's a lovely thought, but it really didn't happen like that, any more than Jesus living in an igloo or wearing the finest Chinese silks. Jesus never had all these luxurious things.

(Enter RUSSIAN and AUSTRIAN.)

Here come two more travellers. Where have you come from?

(NOMAD stands to one side.)

RUSSIAN I'm from Russia…

AUSTRIAN …and I'm from Austria.

RUSSIAN We are looking for the new-born king so we can offer him a place in one of our homes. Our countries are very cold in winter, but we could put plenty of logs on the fire and make it warm for him.

AUSTRIAN My chalet is very beautiful, with flowers in the windows and mountains all around. It is fit for a king.

RUSSIAN I would carve beautiful toys for the king and paint them in bright colours.

NARRATOR That sounds wonderful, but it's just not how it happened when Jesus was born to be king.

(Enter FOOTBALLER.)

Here comes someone else. Who are you?

(RUSSIAN and AUSTRIAN stand to one side.)

FOOTBALL.   I'm a real English football supporter and I've heard a new king has been born. I'd like him to come and live in my house. I could easily get it ready. The neighbours aren't too noisy and I could make a lovely nursery for him to sleep in. When he's bigger I could get him a season ticket to watch the matches. He'd have everything he needed.

NARRATOR   That's a lovely thought, but it really isn't the way things worked out for this baby king.

(Enter HAWAIAN and WELSH.)

Maybe these two can tell us something.

(FOOTBALLER stands to one side.)

WELSH   Can you please help me? I've come from Wales. I've heard a new king has been born. I have a beautiful stone cottage in the hills. I would like to welcome the new king to live in my home. I could wrap him in wool from the mountain sheep. He would be so warm and comfortable.

HAWAIAN   My home is not like that. I am from Hawaii and I live in a grass hut. I would love the new king to live in my home. It is always warm there and he could play in the sand and learn to swim in the sea.

NARRATOR   You are so kind. I think the baby king would have been very comfortable in both of those homes…

(Enter UGANDAN.)

	...but what really happened was very different to all you have said. Who is this colourful person? Where have you come from?

(WELSH and HAWAIAN stand to one side.)

UGANDAN	I am from a village in Uganda. I have a well-swept mud hut where the baby king could live. It's the chief's hut – the very best.
NARRATOR	I'm sorry, but we can't just change what actually happened.
UGANDAN	The king would love our joyful music and the great rhythms. We could beat the drums and invite everyone from the neighbouring villages to welcome him. He would get a real African welcome.
NARRATOR	I don't think that's the way God meant it to be.

(Enter ARAB and TURK.)

	These two look as though they are from the area where Jesus was born. Where have you come from?

(UGANDAN moves aside.)

ARAB	I am from Iran. Some wise men from my country told me that a new king has been born. They have been studying the stars and say that they have seen the sign in the sky of the coming king. I would like to offer him my clean white house, the very best my country has. The roof-top is flat and the king could sleep there when it is not too hot. He would live like our great kings and rulers, with every luxury we can offer him.
TURK	I am from Turkey. I would like the new king to come to my home. I have many beautiful rugs my family make by hand. They are fit for a king to lie on.

NARRATOR   Even that doesn't sound right – luxury homes, beautiful rugs.

(Enter FRENCH.)

It just wasn't like that when Jesus was born. Now here's someone else. Where have you come from?

(ARAB and TURK stand to one side.)

FRENCH   I am from Paris in France. I am looking for the new-born king. I have a flat looking over the River Seine. It is fit for any king. I would like to welcome him to live with me.

NARRATOR   But we all know it didn't happen like that either.

(FRENCH stands to one side.)

The new king wasn't born in a palace, or a luxury flat, or a grass hut, or an igloo. He was never wrapped in silk or Welsh wool. His parents were strangers in Bethlehem and there was no room for them to stay in the inn, so they slept in the stable. It was there that Jesus, the king of kings, was born – a place that smelt of hay and cows and donkeys and...

FOOTBALL.   What was his cot like, then?

NARRATOR   He had no cot. He was put in a manger, the place where the animal's food is normally put. It happened like this.

(Either open the curtains for the reading, or let MARY and JOSEPH enter with baby and place him in the manger.)

READER   *(Read Luke 2:1-7.)*

(ALL gather round manger.)

WELSH   But why? That was no way for God to treat his son.

NARRATOR When God sent his Son to the earth as a baby, he knew that he needed to understand how humans feel. What if he had lived in a palace? He would only have known what it was to be rich and famous. God sent Jesus to live amongst the poor and needy. He even became a refugee when his family fled to Egypt. He came for all people, not just kings in palaces.

The Donkey and the King

Three donkeys are in a field talking together. The littlest one, Little Grey, feels inferior, but does share his greatest wish – to carry a king on his back. The donkeys' owner appears with Joseph and Mary. He asks them to choose one of the donkeys to take them to Bethlehem. The two bigger donkeys jostle for position, leaving Little Grey in the corner. However, it is Little Grey that Mary chooses and so his adventures begin.

This can be played very simply – as a story read by an adult with the action done by younger children.

Alternatively:

1. The story can be dramatized using several readers and with the rest of the children miming.
2. The speech can be taken from the story, dramatizing the whole thing with speaking parts.

CAST

Story reader or readers

Non-speaking Parts

Mary
Joseph
Nathan
Innkeeper

DONKEYS
Hee
Haw
Little Grey

Sheep
Cows
Shepherds
Shepherd boy
Wise men
Wise men's attendants
(optional)

SCENE ONE
In the Donkeys' Field in Nazareth

(DONKEYS stand in field and nuzzle up to each other – there needs to be some movement.)

NARRATOR   Once upon a time, well, over two thousand years ago, three donkeys lived in a field in a town called Nazareth. Nazareth was a small town in a little-known corner of the great Roman Empire.

The donkeys, whose names were Hee, Haw and Little Grey, often saw Roman soldiers riding past their field on fine horses. They looked so proud – the horses whose riders had red and gold helmets, leather boots and shining swords.

'No one like that will ever ride us,' said Hee.

'Fine chance,' said Haw. 'We only carry poor people and their heavy burdens. My back still aches from carrying all that hay last week.'

'I'd love to carry a king,' said Little Grey dreamily. 'Soldiers only fight, but kings – well, everyone would cheer as we went by and I would have silk covers, not the scratchy old sacking that Nathan uses.'

'No king would ever ride on you,' said Haw rudely. 'Look at you – your nose isn't straight and your tail is too short for a respectable donkey.'

'And you're too small to carry a great man like a king,' said Hee.

Little Grey walked away to the other side of the field where there was a small pond. 'I can dream, can't I?' he said to himself. 'After all, who's ever heard of a king riding on a donkey anyway?'

He had reached the pond and, as he looked down into the water, he caught sight of his reflection. Was his nose really crooked? Did he have a shorter tail than all the other donkeys? He was small, he knew that; Hee and Haw were much bigger than him.

This is why, when a few days later the three donkeys were quietly chewing their hay, Little Grey had the biggest surprise of his life.

(Curtain, if possible.)

SCENE TWO
In the Donkeys' Field

(DONKEYS on stage as before. Enter MARY, JOSEPH and NATHAN.)

NARRATOR It all began when two people came along to the donkey's field with Nathan, their boss. The man was kind, the donkeys knew that. He was Joseph, the local carpenter. They had often carried wood for him to his carpenter's workshop and Joseph always gave them hay and carrots as a reward. But the lady – well, she was only a girl, really; they had never seen her before. She must live in Nazareth; she spoke in the same way as Nathan and Joseph, not like the Roman soldiers. The girl was beautiful and had a gentle voice. It was plain to see too that she was expecting a baby.

'What do you think Mary?' Joseph was saying to the girl. 'Could you make it all the way to Bethlehem if we borrowed one of these donkeys? You could ride whenever you needed to – Bethlehem is such a long way.'

'It will be my gift to you and the baby,' Nathan said. 'You can choose which donkey you would like and I will give it to you to keep for your very own.'

The three donkeys heard every word. Hee and Haw jostled each other, trying to outdo one another for the position where the couple would have the best view of them. Little Grey crept away. 'My nose is crooked, my tail's too short and I'm too small even to be noticed,' he said sadly to himself. These kind people may not be kings but he would have been very happy to be their donkey.

By this time, Hee and Haw were almost fighting in their eagerness to be seen. Then Hee lifted his head up and down to show how straight his nose was. Not to be outdone, Haw flicked his tail. He could push away flies as he walked along, not just from himself but from anyone riding him as well.

Joseph and Mary watched all these antics. Hee and Haw were certainly very fine donkeys. They were used to heavy loads and Joseph knew only too well how strong they both were. 'What do you think, Mary?' he asked.

'I like that little one over there,' she answered. 'He looks gentler and more patient than these two. I would be afraid that the bigger ones would go too fast and throw me off when I was riding.'

And so it was that Little Grey was chosen to carry Mary on her journey to Bethlehem.

(Curtain, music.)

SCENE THREE
Bethlehem

(Begin on floor level and on stage for the inn.)

NARRATOR   It had been a long and difficult journey. Mary and Joseph were so kind to Little Grey as he had expected. Mary never rode him for too long and, when she wasn't riding, she walked along beside him, talking to him. She told him about the baby she was expecting – a boy, who was going to be called Jesus, and he was God's son.

Little Grey wondered how she knew all this even before the baby was born.

As Mary spoke to him, Little Grey felt calm and very happy. He wondered how Hee and Haw were getting on, how hard they were working and if they were cross with him for being chosen for this special job.

At last Joseph gave a shout: 'Look, that's got to be Bethlehem ahead. Not much longer now, Mary.'

'Where will we stay?' Mary asked. 'Everyone seems to be going towards Bethlehem today.'

(By this time JOSEPH and MARY should have reached the stage and be going towards the inn door.)

'We'll soon find a place,' said Joseph.

But he was wrong. Little Grey stood patiently as Joseph knocked on yet another door. *(knock on door or hit floor with staff)* Everywhere seemed to be full. Joseph saw the innkeeper shake his head, just as all the others had done before him. Then he stopped. 'There's the stable round the back,' he said. 'It's not much, but it's dry and warm and I can't send your wife away in her condition.'

Joseph turned to look at Mary. 'We'll take it,' he said.

(Exit back of stage, INNKEEPER leading LITTLE GREY.)

The innkeeper led Little Grey, followed by Joseph and Mary.

(Music.)

SCENE FOUR
In the Stable

(Put manger and stool in place. Enter ANIMALS and stand in position.)

NARRATOR   It wasn't a bad place. The animals were a bit noisy. 'Little bit like Hee and Haw,' thought Little Grey, but they were friendly enough. Then he heard another noise, the sound of crying. It was so different from the animal noises. As soon as all the animals heard it they fell quiet.

Joseph and Mary had been gone from the stable for some time and when they came back, Mary was carrying the source of the cries – a tiny baby, wrapped in cloth.

(Enter JOSEPH and MARY carrying the baby, MARY puts baby in the manger.)

Gently she put the baby in the manger which the innkeeper had filled with fresh straw.

Little Grey looked at the couple. They both looked very happy. Then he looked at the baby – he couldn't take his eyes off him. What had Mary told him as they travelled to Bethlehem? This was God's Son. He didn't understand, maybe he never would.

(Enter SHEPHERDS from stage front, YOUNG BOY ahead.)

The animals were still quiet when the door of the stable was gently pushed open. It was a young boy, dressed in the sort of rags worn by shepherds and beggars. 'This is it,' he shouted. 'The angels were right!'

'Sh-h-h-h-h,' went the animals.

'Be quiet, young Aaron,' said a man, equally ill-dressed. 'You'll wake the new-born baby.'

By this time the stable was beginning to get a bit crowded.

(SHEPHERDS kneel.)

Three more men had joined the boy and the first man. 'Yes, shepherds,' thought Little Grey as it was a lamb that one of the men carried. But what were they doing here? Why were they kneeling down beside the manger as if they were worshipping the baby?

'You are welcome,' said Joseph, 'but how did you come to be looking for us? The baby is only a few hours old.'

One of the shepherds stood up. 'It was like this,' he said. 'We were out on the hillside minding our sheep and minding our own business, when an angel appeared out of nowhere and God's glory light shone around us. We were terrified. Then an angel told us not to be afraid because he had good news to tell us. The Saviour had been born in Bethlehem and we'd find him wrapped in cloth and lying in a manger. Before we had time to blink, a whole lot more angels appeared and were singing praise to God. Then the angels went away, and the lights and everything. We were left wondering what to do, but we were curious. We decided to come and see if the angel was speaking the truth.'

Little grey couldn't believe his ears – shepherds, angels, lights. What did it all mean?

(Enter WISE MEN and ATTENDANTS from back of hall.)

His thoughts were interrupted. A new group of people were coming towards the stable. But these were no shepherds. These people were rich, they had servants with them and they looked as though they would feel more at home in a palace.

(WISE MAN 1 reaches stage.)

One of them spoke. Even his voice sounded rich. 'Where is the one who has been born a king?'

'King?' said Little Grey to himself. 'Did he say king?'

(Enter REST OF WISE MEN and ATTENDANTS.)

All the newcomers had entered by now. The three rich men – for there were three of them – looked around. They saw the baby lying in the manger and at once, like the shepherds, they knelt down.

(ALL kneel).

They gave gifts to the baby, placing them beside the manger.

'What strange gifts for a baby,' thought Little Grey. 'Gold, that's kingly anyway; frankincense, that's what the priests use when they pray for the people; myrrh, that's for burial.' His donkey mind tried to work it all out. Suddenly it dawned on him. If this baby Jesus was the Son of God, a baby king, then he had done it! All the way from Bethlehem he had carried a king – no, more than a king.

Little Grey could not have been happier. He thought of his friends back in the field in Nazareth. They had missed all this. Maybe one day he would return to Nazareth and tell them about the new king and the manger and the presents – what news he had to tell!

(ALL cast stay still for a short time, then turn and bow.)

Beyond the Star

Starting with Creation, this follows the theme of stars right through the Old Testament to the wise men and into Revelation. Apart from practising the readers, this play needs very little rehearsing and can be put together in a very short time.

The stars' costumes can be adapted from angels' costumes without the wings and with the addition of stars.

CAST

Stars (6 + according to how many available and size of stage)
Sun
Moon
Abraham
David
Joseph
Mary
Wise man 1
Wise man 2
Wise man 3
Reader 1
Reader 2
Reader 3
Reader 4

BIBLE READERS

One very good reader could manage these readings as none are too long, however there are nine readings so they could be shared out

Card holder

SCENE ONE
Creation

(Scene opens with STARS standing on stage, each holding a black card in front of them.)

READER 1   Have you ever wondered what it would be like if there was no light – no stars, no sun, no candles, no electric lights or any other source of light?

READER 2   Before time began, there was total darkness, not even a glimmer of light.

(STARS hold up black cards to make blanket of darkness.)

READER 3   The first thing God did when he began to create the world was to separate light from darkness, making daytime and night-time.

(STARS divide into two – half still holding black card and other half turn cards round to show white or yellow.)

READER 1   It was not until the fourth day of creation that God said:

(BIBLE READING 1: Read Genesis 1:14-19.)

(STARS put down cards to reveal star costumes. Enter SUN and MOON. MOON and STARS group together, SUN stands alone.)

READER 3   If we look up at the sky on a clear night we can see the moon and stars, but even then it is easy to forget what a huge universe we live in.

READER 4   Just think about this.

(STARS, MOON, SUN sit down to listen.)

The nearest star to us is our sun. It is ninety-three million miles away from the earth.

(CARD HOLDER holds up card saying '93 million miles'.)

It takes nearly eight-and-a-half minutes for light to travel from the sun to us.

(CARD HOLDER holds up card saying '8½ minutes'.)

READER 3   Light travels at one hundred and eighty-six thousand miles every second.

(CARD HOLDER holds up card saying '186,000 miles per second'.)

A light year measures the distance light travels in a year. The next nearest star to our sun is four-and-a-quarter light years away from the earth. An ordinary calculator does not have enough space to work out now many miles that is.

READER 4   Our galaxy is one hundred thousand light years across...

(CARD HOLDER holds up card saying '100,000 light years')

...and contains one to two hundred thousand million stars...

(CARD HOLDER holds up card saying 'Wow!' or similar word.)

...but the Bible tells us...

(BIBLE READING 2: Read Psalm 147:4-5.)

(Exit STARS, MOON, SUN.)

READER 2   After God had created the lights, he created living creatures. Last of all he created human beings – a man and a woman – to be his friends and enjoy the beauty he had made.

READER 1   But the man and the woman disobeyed God and so sin came into the world.

(CARD HOLDER holds up card saying 'sin'.)

From that time on we read in the Bible of the way God worked out his plan to defeat sin so that men and women could once again be his friends.

(Exit CARD HOLDER.)

READER 2   First God needed a nation which would trust him and follow his laws. Every nation begins with one man. God needed a special man if he was to make such a nation. He chose Abraham, who became the very first person in the nation of Israel.

(Enter ABRAHAM and hold up card saying 'nation'.)

READER 1   The book of Hebrews in the Bible tells us that Abraham was a man who knew and obeyed God.

(BIBLE READING 3: Read Hebrews 11:8.)

READER 3   Because he had shown he was faithful, God gave Abraham a promise. At a time when Abraham and his wife Sarah had given up all hope of having children, we read this...

(BIBLE READING 4: Read Genesis 15:5-6a.)

READER 4   Abraham and Sarah did have a son, whom they called Isaac.

(Exit ABRAHAM.)

READER 1   Isaac had a son called Jacob.

READER 2   Jacob had twelve sons who became the first of the tribes of the nation of Israel.

READER 3   And so the nation grew.

READER 4   From time to time, God gave glimpses of his plans for the future of the nation of Israel and for the whole world. A man called Balaam once spoke of Israel saying...

(BIBLE READING 5: Read Numbers 24:17.)

READER 3   As God's plan began to unfold, we find that God not only chose a nation, he also chose a special family from the chosen nation. His next promise was to a king, Israel's greatest king, King David...

(Enter DAVID and hold up card saying 'family'.)

(BIBLE READING 6: Read 2 Samuel 7:8b-9,16.)

READER 2   David was born in a town called Bethlehem, a small, unimportant place quite near to Jerusalem. It was in Jerusalem that David set up his capital and where his son Solomon built the great Temple.

(Exit DAVID.)

READER 1   Kings came and went, the nation went further and further away from worshipping God. Stronger nations defeated the Israelites and destroyed the Temple.

READER 4   But God kept faithfully to his promises. David's family line continued because God needed a special man and woman whom he could trust to bring up his own son.

(Set stage with manger and stool for MARY.)

(Enter JOSEPH and MARY from the back of hall carrying the baby. Come up onto stage and place baby in the manger)

READER 1   God's timing and plans are always just right. The Bible tells us...

(BIBLE READING 7: Read Galatians 4:4-5.)

READER 2   When God's son, Jesus, was born, something strange happened in the sky – a very bright star appeared, so clear that it could be seen by astronomers hundreds of miles away. It shone directly over Bethlehem. The sign that God's Star had come to earth was a bright star in the sky.

(Enter STARS, one carrying a large star. Stand around crib, hold up large star.)

(Suggest song here: 'Light of the World, You Stepped Down into Darkness'.)

READER 3   Astronomers, or wise men, travelled many miles, following the star, to find the reason it had suddenly appeared in the sky.

READER 4   Knowing the words that Balaam had spoken all those years before, they thought they were looking for a baby prince. They went to the palace of King Herod in Jerusalem. Herod's advisors pointed the Wise Men towards Bethlehem.

(BIBLE READING 8: Read Matthew 2:1b-4a,9-11.)

(Sing carol: 'We Three Kings', first and last verses.)

(Enter WISE MEN during singing from back of hall, come slowly down, present gifts and kneel at manger.)

READER 2   But who is the brightest star of all time? It is the God of eternity who lives beyond time. In the last book of the Bible, Jesus says…

(BIBLE READING 9: Read Revelation 22:16b.)

READER 1   Let's see beyond the presents, the decorations and even the star this Christmas, to a baby who became the Saviour of the world, the Bright Morning Star who offers life and peace to all.

Christmas – The Real Story

The story began long before the angel first appeared to Mary, so this play begins with Creation. It is an opportunity to use dance/movement to represent Creation both for an older and a younger group of children and, later on in the play, the stars. A good-size stage is needed and, preferably, curtains and spotlights. It can involve a wide age range of children, but does need someone who can work on the choreography.

CAST

Reading Parts

Narrator 1
Narrator 2
Storyteller

Acting Parts

Mary
Joseph
Gabriel
Innkeeper
Shepherds
Wise Men
Angels
Adam
Eve

Dancers

Older children to represent light and then stars
A soloist for the Nativity Star
Younger children to represent creation

SCENE ONE
Creation

(NARRATORS standing on stage left. If curtains, they remain closed with NARRATORS standing in front. Lights on NARRATORS.)

NARRAT. 1   This is the real story of what happened at the very first Christmas. There were no fairy lights, no Christmas trees or mince pies or puddings. The presents were strange and rather mysterious and the singing was just heavenly!

But let's go back to the very beginning of the story. How did it all start?

NARRAT. 2   With a baby in a manger, wasn't it?

NARRAT. 1   No, it goes back a long time before that; in fact before time began, before God made the universe.

NARRAT. 2   But that's impossible.

NARRAT. 1   Not with God it isn't. God planned from the very beginning to send his son into the world to rescue people from their sin. He wanted all the people he made to know and love him, just as he loves them.

NARRAT. 2   Hang on a minute. When God made the universe, he already knew all about Christmas. Is that how it was?

NARRAT. 1   Well yes, God's plan began to work out when, out of chaos and darkness, he made the most wonderful world – light came out of darkness… *(all lights out)*

(Curtains open to complete darkness, OLDER DANCERS already in position.)

(Movement/dance to music using, for example, glow-sticks or lighted balloons.)

(Lights on, exit OLDER DANCERS.)

(Enter YOUNGER DANCERS representing creation. They can be animals, flowers, sun, moon, or any combination.)

(Movement/dance to suitable music to represent creation itself.)

(YOUNGER DANCERS remain on stage in semicircle, enter ADAM and EVE standing so that they are in the centre of the semicircle.)

NARRAT. 1   God saw everything he had made and he was thrilled with all he saw. But then the trouble began. His crowning part of creation – mankind – disobeyed his command.

(ADAM and EVE hide faces, DANCERS stand still.)

NARRAT. 2   Was that when Adam and Eve ate the fruit of the tree of the knowledge of good and evil?

NARRAT. 1   Yes, and because of that, sin came into the world. But God made a way to overcome sin and set men free to love him.

NARRAT. 2   Is that why he sent Jesus into the world – to deal with the sin problem?

NARRAT. 1   Yes, God sent his son at just the right time in history, to a nation and family he had specially chosen.

NARRAT. 2   And now can we see what happened when Jesus came?

(Curtains close.)

SCENE TWO
The Angel Visits Mary

(Curtains open, lights on stage and spotlight on storyteller.)

(Mary sweeping up on stage.)

STORYTELL.   It was round about the year nought. In an ordinary home in Nazareth, a small town in northern Israel, there lived a young girl called Mary. She was engaged to the village carpenter, a man called Joseph.

One day, Mary was at home, minding her own business, when suddenly a very important angel named Gabriel appeared in the room right in front of her. What a shock!

The angel understood how Mary felt…

(GABRIEL helps MARY to sit down.)

…and spoke gently to her. 'Don't be afraid, Mary. I am bringing you greetings from God. He is with you and has a special work for you to do. You are going to have a son and you are to call him Jesus. He will be the Messiah, the saviour your people have been waiting for all these hundreds of years.'

'But I am not married yet,' said Mary. 'I can't possibly be pregnant.'

Gabriel replied, 'God's Holy Spirit will do what seems impossible. This child will be God's very own son.'

Mary's answer to all this was amazing. 'I am God's servant. I will do whatever he asks of me.'

(Curtains close.)

SCENE THREE
No Room at the Inn

(Action takes place in front of the curtain with spotlight on STORYTELLER and stage front.)

NARRAT. 2   Whatever happened next? Mary's fiancé, Joseph, must have been upset when he discovered that she was pregnant.

STORYTELL. Joseph had a dream and in the dream an angel told him everything that he had told Mary. Joseph knew the baby was to be God's son.

(MARY and JOSEPH begin to walk from back of hall – spotlight on them as they walk down.)

STORYTELL. And so we find Mary and Joseph far away from Nazareth in a place called Bethlehem.

NARRAT. 2 What were they doing there? It must have been a hard journey for Mary.

STORYTELL. They were obeying the Roman rulers who said that everyone was to go to the place their families came from so they could be counted. When Mary and Joseph arrived in Bethlehem, they found it already crowded.

(MARY and JOSEPH on to the stage. JOSEPH knocks at the inn door – centre of curtain.)

STORYTELL. The inn was full up. They must find a place to stay for the night. The baby was soon to be born and Mary was very tired.

(Enter INNKEEPER.)

Mary and Joseph would have slept anywhere that night as long as there was a comfortable place for Mary to lie down. So they ended up sleeping among the animals. It was the best the innkeeper could do.

(INNKEEPER takes MARY and JOSEPH behind curtain. Lights off.)

SCENE FOUR
The Birth of Jesus

(Spotlight on STORYTELLER.)

STORYTELL. After Mary and Joseph arrived in Bethlehem, the baby was born. All their plans for the baby's birth and the lovely crib Joseph had made for the baby were back in Nazareth. All Mary could do was to wrap the baby Jesus in strips of cloth and lay him in the trough where the animals normally fed.

(Music gently playing. Curtains open on a tableau of MARY, JOSEPH and the baby in the manger with the animals from the creation scene standing around. Hold tableau for as long as appropriate – could sing 'Away in a Manger' here or another carol.)

(Curtains and lights off.)

SCENE FIVE
Shepherds in the Hills

(SHEPHERDS sitting around a fire with their sheep, curtain open, dim lighting.)

STORYTELL. Meanwhile, out in the hills near Bethlehem, some shepherds were watching their sheep making sure that nothing scary happened to them.

NARRAT. 2 And the scary thing happened to the shepherds instead.

STORYTELL. You could say that.

(Enter GABRIEL.)

God's special messenger appeared, suddenly and without any warning. The shepherds were terrified.

(SHEPHERDS act terrified.)

The angel told them not to be afraid because he was bringing them good news that the Messiah, the special saviour, had been born in Bethlehem. The angel told them they would find the baby wrapped in strips of cloth and lying in a manger. That would be the sign that what the angel had said was true.

(Enter ANGELS with as much lighting on them as possible.)

STORYTELL. No sooner had the angel spoken than a whole company of angels appeared. It was as though they burst out of heaven. They sang praises to God – heavenly music. The shepherds had never heard anything like it.

And just as suddenly as it started, so it went – the music, the angels and the messenger. What did it all mean?

(Lights fade. SHEPHERDS discuss among themselves.)

STORYTELL. There was nothing else for it, they must go to Bethlehem to see if everything the angel had said was true.

(Exit SHEPHERDS to back of hall. Curtain, lights out.)

SCENE SEVEN
Stars

(Spotlight on STORYTELLER.)

STORYTELL. In those days, just as now, many people studied the stars. Then, there were no electric lights to hide many of the stars. Astronomers could see them in their millions.

(Curtains open, lights, empty stage, enter STARS.)

(Movement/dance to appropriate music.)

(Enter NATIVITY STAR and stand at back of stage. As music fades, STARS move aside and NATIVITY STAR moves forward.)

STORYTELL. At the time Jesus was born, a new star appeared in the sky. It was bigger than any other star and was seen right across the Middle East area.

(NATIVITY STAR to do solo dance to appropriate music.)

(When dance finished, exit STARS. NATIVITY STAR stands at back of stage.)

NARRAT. 2   How do we know that this star appeared?

STORYTELL. Some astronomers, wise men from an eastern country, saw the star.

(Enter WISE MEN, see NATIVITY STAR, discuss what to do.)

STORYTELL. They knew about the promise to God's people that a saviour was going to be born and that there was to be a sign telling of this birth. They knew too that he would be a king, so they travelled to the palace in Jerusalem, thinking they could worship him there.

(NATIVITY STAR leads WISE MEN off stage, down side aisle and waits at back of hall.)

(Curtain, lights off.)

SCENE EIGHT
Shepherds and Wise Men Worship the Baby

(MARY, JOSEPH and ANIMALS at the manger as before, curtains open, lights on.)

NARRAT. 1   The shepherds did go to Bethlehem and found that all the angel had told them was true. The baby was wrapped in strips of cloth and was lying in a manger. Their excitement was unparalleled.

(SHEPHERDS come down central aisle of hall, up on to stage and kneel at side of manger.)

STORYTELL.   Of course, the wise men didn't find the baby in Jerusalem as they had thought. They were directed to Bethlehem. So they followed the star until it stopped over the place where the baby was. Then they worshipped him.

NARRAT. 2   Didn't the wise men bring strange presents with them?

STORYTELL.   They did. They brought three presents. There was gold that showed Jesus was a king. There was frankincense which is a picture for prayer and showed Jesus was God. Then there was myrrh. That represented death – a sign that Jesus would one day die to be the saviour of the world.

(WISE MEN, led by NATIVITY STAR, come down centre aisle, present gifts and kneel in front of manger. This can be done while STORYTELLER is reading.)

(Enter ANGELS and STARS from back stage to make completed tableau for final scene when a carol could be sung or just suitable music played, then faded.)

NARRAT. 1   And that's how it was – the real story of Christmas. The Saviour of the world had no rich parents or fine palace, but a borrowed manger in a town far from home, unrecognised except by a few shepherds and wise men who worshipped him as Lord of all.

Good News – Great Joy

This play is designed to be suitable for a younger group, involving a number of rabbits who dance around the manger and look cute! Adults or older children can do the readings and narration. It is shorter than other plays and simple in approach. It can easily be done without the need for lighting effects or stage curtains.

CAST

Reading Parts	**Miming Parts**

Reading Parts

Reader 1
Reader 2
Narrator

Miming Parts

Mary
Joseph
Innkeeper
Gabriel
Angels
Shepherds
Wise Men
Lots of cute rabbits
A big star is needed above action

SCENE ONE
In Mary's House

(The NARRATOR and READERS are standing at the side of the stage.)

(MARY is sitting on a stool sewing.)

NARRATOR   Our story begins in a simple house in Nazareth.

READER 2   God sent the angel Gabriel to a town in Galilee named Nazareth. He had a message for a young girl promised in marriage to a man named Joseph who was a descendant of King David. The girl's name was Mary.

(Enter GABRIEL.)

READER 1   The angel came to her and said, 'Peace be with you! The Lord is with you and has greatly blessed you.'

(MARY jumps up startled, drops sewing.)

READER 1   Then the angel said to her, 'Don't be afraid, Mary. God has been gracious to you. You will become pregnant and give birth to a son and you will name him Jesus. He will be great and will be called the Son of the Most High God and he will be the king of the descendants of Jacob for ever, his kingdom will never end.'

READER 2   Mary said to the angel, 'I am a virgin, how then can this happen?'

READER 1   The angel answered, 'The Holy Spirit will come on you and God's power will be on you and so the child will be called the Son of God.'

(MARY bows her head.)

READER 2   'I am the Lord's servant,' Mary said. 'Let it happen just as you have said.'

(Exit GABRIEL, then MARY in different direction.)

SCENE TWO
In Bethlehem

NARRATOR   Now we jump over nine months to the next part of the story. During that time Mary married Joseph who was told in a dream that Mary's baby was God's Son and he was to be called Jesus.

Then life suddenly became complicated for the young couple. The Roman Emperor wanted to know how many people were in his empire. He ordered everyone to return to the place where their family came from so they could be counted.

(Enter JOSEPH and MARY from back of hall, come up the centre slowly during reading.)

READER 1   Joseph and Mary travelled from Nazareth to the town of Bethlehem, the birthplace of King David. Joseph was a descendant of David.

(Enter INNNKEEPER doing some sweeping.)

(MARY and JOSEPH reach stage and JOSEPH knocks on the floor with a stick. He asks the INNKEEPER for place to stay. The INNKEEPER shakes head, then has an idea and shows MARY and JOSEPH to the stable.)

(Exit ALL to side of stage.)

READER 1   While they were in Bethlehem, Mary had her baby. She wrapped him in strips of cloth and laid him in a manger – there was no room for them to stay at the inn.

SCENE THREE
In the Stable

(Place stool and manger in centre of stage. You may want to have some cows, sheep, etc. in the stable as well.)

(Enter JOSEPH and MARY carrying baby. Put baby in manger.)

NARRATOR   God's son, Jesus, came down to earth. What must the animals and birds have thought? Did they know that this was God's son? Were animals among the first to see the baby?

(Enter RABBITS from all directions, who peep at the baby and then form a circle around the manger and dance around to suitable music.)

(RABBITS exit.)

NARRATOR   So creation rejoiced and the baby slept.

(Exit MARY and JOSEPH. Clear stage.)

SCENE FOUR
On the Hillside

(Put fire to one side of stage.)

(Enter SHEPHERDS and sit round fire.)

NARRATOR   A bunch of ordinary shepherds were on night duty.

READER 1   There were some shepherds in that part of the country who were spending the night in the fields, taking care of their sheep. Suddenly an angel appeared and they were scared stiff.

(Enter GABRIEL, SHEPHERDS act frightened.)

READER 2   But the angel said to them, 'Don't be afraid. I am here to bring you good news which will bring great joy to all people. Today in David's town your Saviour was born – Christ the Lord. This is what will prove it to you: you will find the baby wrapped in cloth and lying in a manger.'

(Enter ANGELS.)

READER 1   Suddenly a great army of angels appeared, singing praises to God: 'Glory to God in the highest and peace on earth to those with whom he is pleased.'

(Exit ANGELS. SHEPHERDS discuss together and then exit in a different direction.)

SCENE FIVE
In the Stable

(Re-set stable scene with MARY and JOSEPH and baby in manger.)

(Enter SHEPHERDS and bow down.)

READER 1   So the shepherds hurried off and found Mary and Joseph and saw the baby lying in the manger just as the angel had said.

When the shepherds saw him, they told Mary and Joseph what the angel had said about the child.

(Exit SHEPHERDS, rejoicing.)

The shepherds went back singing and praising God for all they had seen and heard.

(Everything else left in place.)

SCENE SIX
Visit of the Wise Men

READER 1   Soon after this, some wise men who studied the stars came asking, 'Where is the baby born to be the king of the Jews? We saw his star when it came up in the east and we have come to worship him.'

(Enter WISE MEN slowly from back of hall.)

READER 2   On their way they saw the same star they had seen in the east. When they saw it, they were very happy as it went ahead of them until it stopped over the place where the child was.

(WISE MEN come up on to stage and present gifts to baby, kneeling down by manger.)

READER 1   When they came to the house, they presented their gifts of gold, frankincense and myrrh. Then they knelt down and worshipped.

(Enter INKEEPER, SHEPHERDS, ANGELS, RABBITS. ALL kneel around manger.)

(Could sing 'Away in a Manger' at this point.)